Sales Scripts That Close Every Deal

Open More Doors. Close More Sales.

Sales Scripts That Close Every Deal

420 TESTED RESPONSES TO 30 OF THE MOST DIFFICULT CUSTOMER OBJECTIONS

Gerhard Gschwandtner

Founder and Publisher of *Selling Power*

with Donald J. Moine, Ph.D.

McGRAW-HILL

New York Chicago San Francisco Lisbon London Madrid Mexico City
Milan New Delhi San Juan Seoul Singapore
Sydney Toronto

1 2 3 4 5 6 7 8 9 0   DOC/DOC   0 9 8 7 6

P/N 147389-0
PART OF
ISBN 0-07-147866-3

McGraw-Hill books are available at special quantity discounts to use as premiums and sales promotions, or for use in corporate training programs. For more information, please write to the Director of Special Sales, Professional Publishing, McGraw-Hill, Two Penn Plaza, New York, NY 10121-2298. Or contact your local bookstore.

 This book is printed on recycled, acid-free paper containing a minimum of 50% recycled, de-inked fiber.

Contents

How to Use This Book

The purpose of this book is to assist you in making more professional, convincing, and effective sales calls; to assist you in closing more sales; and thus to help you and your employer make more money.

Even the best salespeople are inconsistent. Each of us has good days and bad days. Sometimes we are unable to recall our best, most convincing lines. This book will help you perform more consistently and excellently.

Since we are each unique individuals, we each have a unique style of selling. This book brings together the "bests" of many different sales styles, ranging from the friendly and gentle approach to some stronger professional approaches. You do not have to like or use every line in this book. As long as you have several powerfully effective ways of handling each objection or challenge you are likely to encounter, you will be far ahead of the competition and other salespeople.

This is your book. Mark it up. Add new phrases and scripts as you think of them. If you don't write it down, you will lose it! Put stars next to your favorite ways of handling difficult objections.

Give yourself the opportunity to use different words and phrases. Try new sales styles. This will give you greater range and flexibility in handling different styles of customers and prospects. Don't put yourself in a box. Give yourself the opportunity to learn and grow. You will be amazed at how choosing the right words or phrases can make the difference between an "almost closed sale" and a successfully closed sale.

This book does not contain any theories of salesmanship. You have already read many books on salesmanship, and you can get more in bookstores. This book has no fat. This is a book of immediately useful lines, scripts, and answers. It is a book that captures the essence of today's sales geniuses.

Study this book. Become as familiar with all the different ways of handling these objections as you can. Learn how to recall the most powerful and compelling way of handling any objection instantly.

State your sales message with great sincerity and feeling. Never say anything you don't believe in 100 percent. Remember that we can trust people like ourselves. We LIKE people like ourselves. Therefore, talk like your clients and prospects. Speed up your voice a little with the "fast-talker." Slow down your delivery of these lines with the "slow-talker." Appropriately match the volume of your prospect's speech. A loud, booming voice will not impress a soft-spoken person.

Remember, it is not just the words, but also how they are said, that makes one sales presentation completely effective and another unconvincing. Use these scripts the way great actors use scripts. Make the script disappear into your polished delivery, the way a great actor can make a script disappear.

Why should you use this script book? What are the benefits to you?

1. You will close more sales and make more money.
2. You will avoid burnout.
3. You will be more flexible and will be able to handle any type of prospect.

4. These are proven scripts taken from highly successful salespeople.
5. You will be able to handle any objection without fear.
6. You will have more selling energy and more energy at the end of the day.
7. You will be able to make more sales calls.
8. Each sales call will be briefer and more closed.
9. You won't have to stumble to remember what to say.
10. You will sound sincere and professional.
11. You will be more organized.
12. If you are new to sales, your training will take less time and less effort.
13. Your persuasive powers in all area of life will compound.
14. Research shows that virtually all sales superstars use scripts. Join them!
15. You will have more fun in selling.

Use this book. Add to it. Improve upon it. Mark it up. Get involved with it. Remember that while it is your book, it is not to be photocopied or reproduced in any way. Know where your book is at all times. You don't want your competition to get their hands on your most powerful sales approaches.

This book will increase your self-confidence. Use it to achieve excellence in all areas of your life. These scripts have helped our client companies bring in millions of dollars in new sales in short periods of time. If you use them, they can work for you.

Your Sales Script Book

Through our studies and work with numerous sales organizations around the world, we have learned that even the best salespeople can be inconsistent. We have observed that even sales geniuses have good days and bad days. On some days, even these top people are unable to remember their own best lines.

Script books (or as they are now called, "sales strategy books") help us perform at peak levels no matter what kind of day we've had. Even if we are tired, if we have our very best lines at our fingertips, we can make some additional calls. We at first doubted the power of sales script books. You may ask yourself, shouldn't salespeople be able to memorize all of their best lines? It hardly seems possible. Time after time, sales superstars themselves rely on script books, and we became convinced of the value of this sales tool. It was no mere coincidence that these highly successful professionals use script books. The script books are, in fact, largely responsible for their success! On those occasions when sales superstars misplace their script books, performance suffers. Imagine a pro football player trying to play without a play book!

The script book makes the job of selling much easier and less stressful. Tom Olds, CPA, sells tax-favored investments to wealthy clients in Orange County, California. Using his script book, he is able to make over 100 phone calls per day! Long after most of his competitors are exhausted and ready to call it quits, Tom still has the energy to make an additional 20 or 30 calls. Late in the afternoon, Olds might come upon any one of dozens of objections, stalls, or resistances from a potential client. He quickly turns to that section of his script book and glances down at a beautiful variety of powerfully persuasive ways of handling the objection. While his competitors are racking their brains to come up with a response, Olds has the most awesome lines in the business at his fingertips. It is no accident that his personal income has increased from $38,000 a year to over $500,000 today.

How Do I Use This Script Book?

Of course, you can't read from a script book word-for-word. Success in sales depends not just upon **what** is said, but also upon **how** it is said. Even Shakespeare's dramatic words lack power and appeal if delivered by someone who doesn't understand projection and pacing.

THE KEY TO DELIVERING THE LINES IS TO SAY THEM JUST THE WAY THE SALES SUPERSTARS SAY THEM. With the proper training, you can read from the script book, and no one will ever suspect you are reading. You will perform like the great actors. When they are acting, we get so caught up in the drama, we never know if they are reading from cue cards or reciting from memory—and we don't care.

For this reason, acting and voice-change techniques are a part of *Selling Power*'s script book training. While this training is a great crowd pleaser, it has a quite serious purpose. Extensive research has shown that we trust people like ourselves. We trust people who sound like we sound. Sales champions know this intuitively. Systemic studies show conclusively that they match their voices to the customer's voice. They will speak slowly to someone who speaks slowly. They will speed up their speech rate with a faster talker. Research shows they will speak softly with people who speak softly. They speak more forcefully with people who have strong voices. When you talk like the other person, the effect is hypnotic. As a result, your closing ratio will skyrocket.

These same powerful scripts can be used in face-to-face selling. Sales script books are not just for telephone sales. They can be very effective memory enhancers for personal sales calls. Here is how to use them.

Suppose you are going to call on Dr. Goodenough. From your first phone call, you know that his major objections will be price, ease of use, and equipment reliability. You drive out to see him one week later. You park outside his office and, before you go in, you look at the following sections of your script book: "Your Price Is Too High," "It's Too Complicated," and "I Don't Want to Take Big Risks." There, at your fingertips, you find the most powerfully persuasive lines you or any other salesperson has ever uttered on these subjects. You glance at them to recharge your memory. They are now on the tip of your tongue. You walk into Dr. Goodenough's office totally relaxed and self-confident. When he brings up these objections, you handle them effortlessly. You make the sale.

Many sales professionals do face-to-face selling almost exclusively and they find that script books are indispensable. They use them every day. One client calls his script book "the brains on the front seat of my car." While nobody reads a script book while directly in front of a client, reviewing the book beforehand is the best investment of two minutes a sales professional can ever make.

Can a Script Book Help Me Be More Creative?

People who do not understand script books sometimes think they will lessen creativity or spontaneity. Our experience clearly demonstrates otherwise. Salespeople who do not use script books are much less creative than those who do know how to use them! More structure actually allows the user more flexibility. Here's how it works.

Many salespeople suffer from insecurity about their persuasive skills. This insecurity leads them to give up too early on sales calls. When they find a line or approach that seems to work, they use it over and over again. The insecurity causes a loss of creativity and a rigidity in their approach.

Some salespeople become superstitious over lines. Just because a line worked once, or some canned sales program said to use it, they say it over and over. They become like robots programmed to say the same thing again and again. "After all," they think, "it worked once. Maybe it will work again." Also, using the same old material seems easier than thinking up new lines, but one pays a huge price in terms of lost income and lost self-confidence.

The sales script book encourages creativity and spontaneity because instead of having just two or three ways of handling an objection, there are dozens of ways. If you want a soft, friendly approach, you have it. If you want a stronger approach, you have it too. If you want to answer the prospect's question with a probing question of your own, there it is at your fingertips. This script book contains logical answers, funny answers, and everything in-between.

With all these approaches and sales styles to select from, salespeople don't grow stale and don't burn out. They find their work fresh and challenging for they always have a new or creative way of handling any objection or closing any sale.

Take humor: Some of the lines in this script book can be funny or even a little zany. These lines can be a great joy to use, and they are also very effective. Some prospects can withstand tremendous pressure, but if you get them to laugh, it will break them wide open! It will totally change the emotional climate. For example, for the "I want to sleep on it" objection, the response, "Okay, but the mattress of missed opportunity is a hard one" consistently breaks the resistance for one stockbroker.

If you think of or hear anything especially new, creative, or dazzling, you can include it in this script book. Extra lines are included in each section to make this easy to do. In addition, this book includes a customizable CD-ROM. Combined with the many different methods of voice-change, voice-matching, and delivery techniques, the sales script book is perhaps the greatest tool available for increasing sales creativity and sales profits.

The Customized Sales Script Book

To produce the highest quality script book, customize it using the enclosed CD-ROM. However, just as few companies today do all of their own legal work or advertising work, few would try to tackle a full-blown script book project. It would be more expensive and more time-consuming to do it in-house, and the finished product would not produce the effective results full-time experts could produce.

To be effective, a customized script book must be based upon research. Sitting in your armchair and dreaming up ways of handling objections and challenges may be fun, but it will not produce a good script book.

To customize your sales script book, tape-record your company's sales superstars in action. This is a priceless aid in building sales script books. When you have captured the exact words of the sales superstars, you have created the foundation of your powerful customized sales script book. Your sales script book will contain knowledge, insights, and techniques not available in any sales book or library in the world!

Do Customized Sales Script Books Produce Even Higher Sales?

Yes, they do. Here is the example: First Federal Savings and Loan of Kalamazoo, Michigan. They developed a customized script book for the purpose of selling First Federal's stock to the public. In one month, First Federal sold over 1,760,000 shares of stock to the public and brought in nearly $14 million! W. David Hamilton, the vice-president and marketing director for First Federal, wrote, "We actually exceeded our estimates of community stock sales, saving a good deal in commissions which would otherwise be paid to underwriters in the national offering." The stock, by the way, has performed very well, and investors have earned over 40 percent profit in less than a year.

The sections in your customized script book, of course, will differ from those of other clients. You might have some similar sections, since nearly all of us in sales must deal skillfully with objections and stalls such as, "I Want to Think About It," and "I

Need to Talk to _____ About It." However, the customized parts of your script book will be quite different.

Customized script books are so effective because they are totally adapted to your particular business. They are powerful because they are based on what your top salespeople actually say, and how they say it. They contain only the proven best lines of your Olympic sales champions, boiled down to their essence, and further enhance your salespeople's effectiveness through extensive training and coaching to make your team thoroughly familiar with your customized sales script book. Imagine how much more profits your company will make with every average performer using the same scripts as your top sales producers!

OBJECTION #1

Attention-Getting Scripts

1. Would you like to have an extra $700 profit per month?

2. Does the idea of increased profits next year appeal to you?
Can I show you a way you can definitely increase your profits?

3. The reason I'm calling is to suggest a way you can add 18 percent or more to your production capacity without a cost increase. Are you interested in that?

4. How important is it to you to keep your employees motivated? May I show you a proven method used by dozens of Fortune 500 companies?

5. If I could show you a way to significantly cut your repair bills, would you be interested?

6. We have been helping companies like yours save time and money with a simple, but unique, device. Would you like to hear about it?

7. I would appreciate the opportunity to learn more about your company's_____ needs. Could you tell me how you rate the product you're using now?

8. Are you familiar with Mr. _____ in _____? He owns _____ Corporation and he's a member of your club. He felt that you would benefit from our services. May I tell you what we do?

9. I read an article about your company in _____ magazine. It says that you're increasing your capacity by 50 percent next year. I'd like to be the first to congratulate you, and I'd like to offer my services to help you with your _____ needs.

10. Thank you for taking the time to sit down with me to discuss your present business situation. In order to be able to help you with your _____ needs, I'd like to ask you a few questions. Okay?

11. If there were an ideal product to solve your problems, what features would you be looking for? **(Now describe your product, emphasizing the features the prospect has just mentioned.)**

12. How do you feel every April 15, when taxes are due? Well, our investors celebrate! Would you like to know why?

13. Have you read about us in _____ magazine?

Did you read the article _____ newspapers did on us?

Would you like to know why we are receiving so much publicity?

14. Would you like to know why our products are called the Rolls Royces of the industry?

Did you know they are available at Chevrolet prices?

15. Have you heard about the special promotion we are having this week only?

Would you like to know how you can save over 50 percent off our regular prices by doing business with us now?

16. _____
_____
_____

17. _____
_____
_____

OBJECTION #2

Getting Through the Secretary

1. I am with _____. This call is about your company's next financial statement. It is very important that I talk to _____. Will you put me through, please?

2. First of all, I am not calling to sell your boss on anything in this phone call. His/her accountant (or lawyer, dentist, banker, tennis partner, chiropractor, doctor, etc.) asked me to get in touch with him/her about a very specific problem. Will you put me through please?

3. Who am I talking to?

Well, _____, you are doing a great job. I want to compliment you on that. I wish my secretary was as thorough as you are.

Please put me through to your boss now. I'm sure she/he will thank you for doing so, because this is a very important matter.

4. Who am I speaking to?

Well, _____, I appreciate your diligence.

I know you must get a lot of calls from people who want to waste your boss' time.

I want to tell you this is not one of those calls.

This is a brief, very important business call.

I appreciate your diligence, but it's not needed in this case.

Your boss will be very grateful if you connect us.

5. What is your last name?

Well, Mr./Ms. _____, you are certainly a very responsible person.

I wish our office staff did the kind of job you do!

But, let me ask you one question: Does your boss want you to screen out important opportunities to save money?

Are you willing to take the **responsibility** of denying your boss this opportunity?

I know he/she will be very grateful if you connect us now. Thank you.

6. I appreciate you being interested in the nature of this call. If I told you about a very specific way to increase your company's productivity by 28 percent, your boss would probably want to know about it, don't you think?

7. You say your boss is extremely busy?

I understand, because I am extremely busy myself.

That's why I'd like you to suggest a specific time when you feel your boss will be less pressured.

Would this afternoon be better, or perhaps first thing at 8:00 a.m. tomorrow?

8. I am returning his call. Please connect us.

9. I am calling long distance. Please connect us.

10. I will be out of the office the rest of the week. This is our only chance to talk. Please connect us.

11. He requested some information in a recent letter to us. I am honoring his request. Please connect us.

12. It will be impossible for her/him to call me back. I travel all the time. What would be the best time for me to reach her/him?

13. This is the _____ time I have tried to get through to him.

Time is running out on this important opportunity. If I can't talk to him/her today, he/she may not have a chance to take advantage of this opportunity.

I'm sure you wouldn't want him/her to miss out on at least hearing about this. Could you please connect us?

14. <u>This call will take less than two minutes of his/her time.</u>

Would you please connect us?

15. Has your boss ever thanked you for putting someone through?

This may be another one of those times. Can you please connect us?

16. I talked with my Congressional Representative this morning.

Why can't I talk with your boss?

17. Would it be better if I just showed up in person?

Should I send a fax?

Wouldn't it be easier and make more sense if you just connected us?

18. I am not a high-pressure person. There is nothing to fear.

Please connect us.

19. _____

_____

_____

20. _____

_____

_____

OBJECTION #3

"Your Price Is Too High."

1. Which means?

2. **Compared to what?**

3. How much did you think it would cost?

4. If our competitor is much less, what does that tell you?

   Perhaps they know how much their product is worth.

5. You know that our quality is the highest you can find, which means that you pay much less over the life of the product. Doesn't that interest you?

6. It is high compared to what some companies charge.

   However, we sell over 800 units a month.

   Why do you think that is?

Do you think these 800 businesspeople would buy from us if they didn't see the superior quality and the value they receive?

7. It costs only about 48 cents per hour of operation.

That's less than a can of Coke out of a vending machine.

You can afford that, can't you?

8. Our price is high compared to what some other companies in this field charge.

But, I believe it's not high enough for what it does.

As a matter of fact, we're expecting an increase any day.

Why not buy now and get our high quality at today's price?

9. I am glad you mentioned price.

That's really the best part about buying from us.

We'll translate the purchase price into small installment payments, so your actual cost per month will be lower with us than with almost any other company!

Can we place an order for you today?

10. Have you ever figured the price of not having high quality?

The price of breakdowns, the cost of wasted time, the extra phone calls, the headaches, the repair bills . . .

<u>You see, the higher quality actually saves you money in the long run. Why not order today?</u>

11. Don't be deceived by today's price.

You actually pay less because we give you more.

More service, more quality, more expertise, more security.

Isn't that what you are really interested in?

12. You really feel that our price is too high? Could you explain that?

13. The sweetness of low price is quickly forgotten when you have to deal day after day with the bitterness of low quality.

14. We can lower the price right now, but you need to make a decision on what options to cut from our proposal. Okay?

15. I might get into trouble for saying this, but I know a way to save you a few bucks.

What if I cut my commission on this transaction to lower the price?

Would that close the deal today?

16. Yes, we are not the cheapest in our field, however, we do over $12 million a year at these same prices.

We couldn't do that if our customers weren't convinced that this is the best buy.

Wouldn't you like to join the ranks of our happy customers?

17.

Does your company pay you only to buy the cheapest products?

Aren't they really interested in your **getting the best value for the dollar?**

Shall we talk about value?

18.

Our price is too high?

We very rarely hear that!

What do you mean?

19.

What kind of car do you drive?

Gee, that is a nice car.

You are obviously a person who appreciates quality.

Why are you trying to cut corners now?

20. What neighborhood do you live in?

That's a nice neighborhood.

You are obviously a person who appreciates the finer things in life.

Why are you denying yourself top quality now?

Does that make sense?

21. <u>How high "too high" is it?</u>

Do you realize that if you keep and use our product for five years, and most people do, that is a price difference of only ten cents a day?

Isn't it worth ten cents a day to have the very best?

22. If it were cheaper, would you want it?

Good!

Then what you are telling me is that you do want it!

Let's look at some ways you can afford it!

23. Why do you think our competitors are cheaper?

Where do you think they cut the corners?

Did they use cheaper materials?

Poorly trained craftsmen?

Did they cut back on quality control?

Why worry about where they cut corners?

Why not buy the best and sleep well at night!

24. _____
_____
_____

25. _____
_____
_____

TION

OBJECTION #4

"I Am Too Busy to Talk with You."

1. JUST AS MUCH AS YOU BELIEVE IN THE VALUE OF YOUR TIME, I BELIEVE IN THE VALUE OF OUR PRODUCT.

I also believe we can save your company a lot of money.

If you are willing to invest only seven minutes, I may be able to help you save $700 or even $7,000.

Would you like to know more?

2. <u>If you were not busy, I would not have invested the long hours to condense my presentation to the five most essential points.</u>

It will take no more than five minutes to cover them.

Can we go over them now?

3. Are you too busy to make more money?

4. (<u>Prospect's name</u>), when you receive a fax, you take the time to read it, don't you? (<u>Wait for yes.</u>)

OBJECTION # 4

Well, think of this phone (sales) call as a very important fax!

The idea I would like to show you doesn't take more than three minutes to explain.

I'm convinced you'll be glad you invested the time!

5. I understand your concern for time.

<u>That's exactly why I want you to be aware that every minute you spend with me now could mean several hundred dollars in your pocket in the future.</u>

I can prove it right here and now, if you give me three minutes. Okay?

6. If you are very busy, then you are just the person I want to see.

It's the busy executive who quickly realizes the value of what we have to offer.

If you had said you had a full hour to talk to me, I would have been less than interested in talking with you.

Our products are designed for the go-getters who appreciate the value of time.

7. (Prospect's name), would you say that to a customer who came to see you with an important purchase order? (Wait for response.)

My point is that I represent just as much a money-making opportunity to you as any one of your customers.

I might be able to make you more money with my product than you could make with your next five customers.

Would you like to know how?

8. If your banker came in to see you and said, "I have a 100 percent safe investment that will pay you 20 percent on your money," you would probably want to give him/her a few minutes to look over his/her proposal. Right?

Now, I have a service that will pay you more than 20 percent on your investment every year.

All I ask is for a few minutes of your time to show you the facts. May I proceed?

9. I can empathize with the position you are in.

You **do** sound very busy, and to you this might seem like just another interruption.

However, I'd like to share with you that this is not like any other calls you may get this week.

This is important business relating to your company's productivity.

If we absolutely cannot talk now, when can we talk?

Please remember that this can't be put off for too long without some risk of loss of productivity.

10. (<u>Prospect's name</u>), if you saw a $100 bill lying on the sidewalk, would you have the time to stop and pick up that bill?

Giving me a moment of your time will be as productive as picking up 10 or even 15 hundred-dollar bills.

11. You are a very busy person.

I am a very busy person.

We understand each other.

Can I have five minutes to show you something that could save you hundreds or perhaps thousands of dollars?

12. You are very busy?

Good!

<u>Let me show you a way you can save a tremendous amount of time!</u>

13. <u>How much time do you think I need?</u>

<u>It is only five minutes!</u>

OBJECTION #4

I'm sure you can invest five minutes to reduce your operating expenses by thousands of dollars, can't you?

14. You remind me of Mr. _____ in

_____.

He thought he was too busy to talk with me.

I couldn't get through to him.

After he heard from some business associates how much money we saved them, **he ended up calling me!**

As long as we are already on the phone, would you like to learn how we save businesses a great deal of money?

15. You are too busy to talk with me?

We very rarely hear that!

It is usually other businesses that call us!

Would you like to know why?

16. You want me to send you some information?

It would take you an hour to read the literature.

If you are really pressed for time, we should talk now.

I can give you the highlights in five minutes.

That will save you 55 minutes over reading about it.

Can we discuss it now, to save you some time?

17. I am glad to hear you are a busy person.

Busy people are our best customers.

They really appreciate our products and services!

Can I tell you why?

18. **We always find time for what is really important, don't we?**

When you tell me you don't have any time, I know what you are really saying is that you don't think this is important, correct?

Can I tell you why over one thousand businesses think we are one of the most important services they use?

19.

You say you don't have any time to talk to me?

We always have time for the things that are really important, don't we?

I know that what you are really saying is that you don't know enough about what we do to understand why it is so important.

May I have a few minutes to explain the importance of our services?

20.

WHAT COULD POSSIBLY BE MORE IMPORTANT THAN LEARNING

HOW YOU CAN SAVE YOUR
COMPANY THOUSANDS OF
DOLLARS??

21. WHAT COULD POSSIBLY BE MORE
IMPORTANT THAN LEARNING HOW
YOU CAN HELP YOUR COMPANY
MAKE THOUSANDS OF DOLLARS IN
ADDITIONAL PROFIT?

22. _____

_____

_____

23. _____

_____

_____

OBJECTION #5

"I'm Too Busy; Talk to Our Purchasing Manager First."

1.

(<u>Prospect's name</u>), suppose you receive a letter marked **"Personal and Confidential."**

Would you allow your purchasing manager to open it? (<u>Wait for a reply.</u>)

The proposal I have was intended for your eyes only.

What I have to say is too important to be shared with anyone outside the executive suite.

Can we talk now?

2.

I appreciate how busy you are.

However, the opportunity I have to share with you will have a significant impact upon the future of your company.

ALL I ASK FOR IS A BRIEF MOMENT TO EXPLAIN THE DOLLAR CONSEQUENCES OF THIS IMPORTANT PROPOSAL.

Isn't this worth a few minutes of your time?

OBJECTION # 5

3. Does he have the authority to approve a
$_____ purchase?

(If the prospect says yes:) Thank you, I'll
be sure to remind him/her and I'll see
him/her right now.

(If the prospect says no:) Well, then,
why should I talk with him/her?

4. Our proposal is really very significant. It
requires detailed information from top
management.

Is _____ privy to all the details
and operating plans known to top
management?

If not, then we should set aside five
minutes to cover the key parts of this
opportunity together.

After that, if you want me to, I will be
happy to talk with _____.

5. ARE YOU TOO BUSY TO SAVE
MONEY?

6. If this opportunity **saves** your company $_____, who do you want to be the hero, you or the purchasing manager?

7. We almost never deal with purchasing managers.

> This is an executive-level decision.
> I need to talk with you.

8. I am sure your purchasing manager is very competent.

> However, I can assure you, this information is beyond her/his realm of expertise.
> This information is for the person who is in charge of the total bottom-line profitability of the company.

9. I cannot talk with purchasing managers.

> It is company policy.
> I will either talk with you, or no one in your company will learn of this opportunity.
> CAN WE TALK?

10. You want me to talk with your purchasing manager?

I know what you are really saying is that you don't think this opportunity is worthy of your attention.

May I have two minutes to explain to you why it is??

11. You want me to talk with someone else?

Why do you think I called you?

It wasn't by chance!

The information I have is for you only!

After you have heard it, if you want me to talk with _____, I will be happy to.

But, I am confident it won't be necessary.

12. How do you feel when you call someone and they ask you to speak with someone else?

Well, that's the way I feel now!

What would you do if you were in my position?

13. Thank you for your suggestion.

The news I have is very important.

WHY DON'T YOU GIVE HIM/HER MY NAME AND NUMBER, AND HAVE HIM/HER CALL ME?

I don't normally talk with purchasing managers.

I'd really prefer to talk with you.

May I have a few minutes of your time?

14. <u>I have already talked with your purchasing manager.</u>

He said it was very important that you and I talk directly.

15. BY HANDING ME OVER TO YOUR PURCHASING MANAGER, WHAT YOU ARE REALLY TELLING ME IS THAT **YOU DON'T KNOW HOW CRITICAL THIS MATTER REALLY IS.**

Would you like to learn why?

OBJECTION # 5

16. _____

_____

_____

17. _____

_____

_____

OBJECTION #6

"It's Too Complicated."

1. MY JOB IS TO MAKE IT EASY FOR YOU.

It will take me only a few minutes to help you and your staff feel like experts.

Shall we proceed?

2. What exactly is it about this product that seems complicated?

3. I AM SURPRISED TO HEAR THAT.

There is no need to worry.

We're going to make it easy for you to understand us and our product.

This product is as easy to use as a TV.

4. If it were too complicated, nobody would be able to use it.

You'll be surprised that it doesn't take a high school diploma to understand this product.

It may look complicated, but it's actually very simple to use.

5. Are you concerned about the time it will take to learn how to use it?

It takes surprisingly little time.

THINK OF ALL THE TIME OUR MACHINE WILL SAVE YOU, ONCE IT IS SET UP IN YOUR OFFICE!

6. It is too complicated?

So is the human body, but as you know, it's actually very easy to use.

7. You know, at one time, people thought indoor plumbing was complicated.

You and I know it's very simple.

Once you have used our product for a little while, you would no more consider going back to any other than you would want to switch to outdoor plumbing.

8. It is too complicated?

Compared to what?

9. <u>What kind of work do you do?</u>

That is very difficult work.

I admire you.

It takes a lot of intelligence and education to do that.

Since you have the intelligence to master your difficult profession, I know you will find that learning how to use our product is a breeze!

10. Listen, I am not a real smart person.

I didn't do that well in school and I am not much of a reader.

<u>If I can learn how to use the product, I am sure it will be a snap for someone like you!</u>

11. YOU KNOW, WE HAVE MANY KIDS WHO ARE 11 OR 12 YEARS OLD WHO LEARN HOW TO USE OUR PRODUCT!

If these kids can learn how to use it, I am certain you can!

OBJECTION # 6

12. Do you remember what it was like trying to learn to drive a car?

It was pretty complicated, wasn't it?

Now, you can probably drive and read a map at the same time.

The point I am making is that <u>many things that seem complicated at first become incredibly simple once you learn how to do them.</u>

It is the same with learning how to use our product!

13. You remind me of Mr. _____ in

_____.

He thought it would be too difficult to learn to use our product.

He thought it would take him weeks to master it.

But, he knew he needed it, and he bought it anyway.

He learned how to use it in less than four hours!

Why don't you buy one today?

I think you will make the same discovery that Mr. _____ made.

14. That is the great thing about buying our product!

We are the only company in the business that includes free training sessions!

You can go back to the training class as many times as you want, free of charge, until you are a master!

However, most of our customers find that one class is all they need.

Why not buy today and we will get you enrolled in the next class?

15. That is the great thing about buying our product!

<u>We are the only company in the industry with a toll-free 800 line to answer all your questions!</u>

I think you will find it very easy to learn how to use our product, but if you ever have any questions, you can call up our in-house experts and they will immediately give you the information you need!

16. _____

_____

_____

17. _____

_____

_____

OBJECTION #7

"I Don't Want to Take Big Risks."

1. You feel it's too risky?
  We very rarely hear that.
  What do you mean by "risky"?

2. "Risky" compared to what?

3. <u>Let's face it, everything in life involves some
  risk, doesn't it?</u>
    We've worked hard to minimize the risk,
  so you can feel safe in buying our product.
    Our up-time rate is over 97 percent!

4. WHAT COULD WE DO TO MAKE YOU
  FEEL MORE SECURE?

5. There is no need to worry about risking your
  money.
    First, we guarantee our product.
    If it should develop a problem, we'll fix it.
    Second, we guarantee that it will do the
  job.
    <u>If it doesn't, we'll return your money.</u>

Third, you can talk to any one of hundreds of our customers who have felt safe and secure with us for the last five years.

You see, there is almost no risk in buying from us!

6. (Prospect's name), it may be **more risky** for you not to buy.

What is the price you may pay for low productivity in your plant?

7. Nothing in life is risk-free.

You know that over half of all marriages end up in divorce.

Is that a good reason for people to give up entirely on marriage?

Of course not!

There is a minimal risk in buying our product.

Why don't we focus on the many benefits of buying our product?

8.   HAVE YOU GIVEN UP ON TAKING ALL RISKS?

9.   That's exactly why I suggest that you make the investment now.

There is risk in all investments.

<u>Even a 5 percent bank passbook isn't guaranteed. We know that banks do fail.</u>

This is the safest time to invest in the market.

All the economic factors say that the opportunity for reward is greatest now and the possibility of loss is very, very low.

Why not invest today?

10.   Well, it may just come down to the fact that you're not comfortable with this right now.

Let me ask you some questions.

When you first learned to drive a car, did you feel comfortable?

When you got your first job, did you feel comfortable?

<u>Did you ever start anything that you felt comfortable with the first day?</u>

No.

Well, this is no different.

I KNOW THAT IN A COUPLE OF WEEKS, YOU WILL FEEL VERY COMFORTABLE AND PROUD OF THIS DECISION.

Why not buy today?

11.

We realize that this seems like a risky decision to you.

For that reason, we are prepared to work twice as hard to keep you satisfied.

12.

Have you ever, ever in your life taken a risk that worked out well?

You are in the same position today.

Take advantage of this opportunity!

13.

You impress me as an intelligent person.

I am a little surprised that you don't see how safe this purchase decision is.

What specific areas are you still concerned about?

14. You think it is too risky to buy our product?

<u>We have the best safety history of anyone in our business!</u>

15. _____

_____

_____

16. _____

_____

_____

OBJECTION #8

"I Want to Work with a More Established Company."

1. You impress me as a very smart businessperson.

I know you haven't invited me here to chat about the weather.

YOU DON'T WANT TO PUT ALL YOUR EGGS IN ONE BASKET, DO YOU?

2. I understand how safe you feel about a relationship that goes back 15 years.

And yet, I saw your eyes light up when you looked at our products.

I can see that you're giving serious consideration to diversity.

Just out of curiosity, could we compare the pros and cons of the two choices?

Let's take a piece of paper and list the reasons for and against buying from us.

The first reason against us is that we haven't worked with you for the past 15 years.

What would be the reasons for giving us a chance to prove ourselves?

3. Is there anything about me that prevents you from doing business with our company?

4. I can only say good things about my competitor and if I were you, I would go with them—unless, of course, you want a better product at a better price.

5. I do respect your loyalty to your present vendor.

Loyalty is a virtue.

While we're on the subject, how about your loyalty to your company's long-term profits?

ISN'T THAT KIND OF LOYALTY JUST AS IMPORTANT AS LOYALTY TO AN OUTSIDE VENDOR?

If I could show you a way of improving your company's profits, would you take a serious look at our products?

6. If I can show you three good reasons why you should change, would you be ready to make a decision right now?

(<u>If the client says yes:</u>)

I'm glad you're being objective about this decision.

Although we're similar in design, when you look closer, you can see three important differences.

First, we have **better quality.**

Second, we can offer you **more selections.** Look at our catalog.

The third, and most important, reason for going with us is that we have the best service record of any company in this industry.

Aren't high quality, more choices, and better service the most important criteria in making a purchase decision??

7. If I can show you **three good reasons** why you should change, would you be ready to make a purchase decision now?

(If the prospect says no:)

Obviously you must have a reason for saying that.

Would you mind telling me what it is?

8. I respect the fact that you have been doing business with another company for many years.

The great majority of our customers have been with us even longer.

Would you like to know why our thousands of customers are so loyal to us??

9. I am happy to hear that you have been doing business with another company for many years.

That is good news for you.

What it means is that we will have to work harder than ever to make sure you are pleased with our products and services!

And, we are prepared to do just that!

Why not give us a try?

10. I respect the fact that you have been doing business with someone else for many years.

I am not asking you to give up that relationship.

We are not asking for all your business.

Just give us a small percentage of it.

You will be happy you did!

11. I am not asking for all your business.

Just give us 1 percent.

WE WILL EARN THE OTHER 99 PERCENT!

12.

You remind me of Mr. _____ in

_____.

He was loyal to another company for 20 years.

Then, he decided to give us a try!

He says it was the best decision he ever made!

Why not give yourself a chance to discover what Mr.

_____ discovered!

13.

You are loyal to another company?

You think you are satisfied with them??

You don't know what satisfaction is until you try us!

Let us show you how **you can be happy,** not just satisfied, by having the highest quality at the lowest prices available!

Can we place a small order today?

14. _____
_____
_____

15. _____
_____
_____

OBJECTION #9

"I Plan to Wait Until Fall."

1.
I understand that you need more time to think.

What are your reasons for and your reasons against buying now?

2.
WE VERY RARELY HEAR THAT.

Why would you delay making this important decision?

3.
Perhaps I can help you.

I am aware that this is an important decision for you.

What do you think you will gain if you buy in the fall, and **what are you going to lose by waiting?**

4.
Are you saying that you wouldn't be able to use the product right now?

No.

Then why wait until fall?

Why not start benefiting today??

5. WHAT WILL CHANGE THEN?
PROBABLY NOTHING.

Your need might even be greater.

If we can solve your problems today, why delay?

6. What will change then?

Probably nothing, except our prices might be higher.

Why not buy today, and take advantage of the low price??

7. **You impress me as a very proactive businessperson.**

You make bigger decisions than this every day.

Why are you hesitating now?

8. You remind me of Mr. _____ in

_____.

He planned to wait several more months before buying our equipment.

Unfortunately, his company didn't have the luxury of waiting.

During those months, they lost their competitive edge.

The competition had new machinery and they didn't.

They lost a lot of business.

I would hate to see anything like that happen to you.

Why not buy today and get ahead of the competition?

9. If your kid needed medical care, would you put it off?

Of course not!

Well, why delay on this purchase decision?

Aren't we in a similar position?

Your company needs this machinery very badly.

Let's get it in place now, so that you can correct this productivity problem now.

10.
Are you in the habit of putting off important decisions?

Isn't it time you broke that habit?

11.
Do you promise me you will definitely buy in the fall?

Good!

I will call you in the middle of the summer so that we can set it up!

12.
You will buy in the fall?

So, what you are telling me is that you definitely want it, right?

Well, let's fill out the paperwork today.

We can arrange to have it shipped to you this fall, okay?

13.
You want to wait until this fall?

Is it just a matter of money?

If that is all it is, we can arrange to have it shipped today, and we won't start billing you until this fall. Okay?

14. _____
_____
_____

15. _____
_____
_____

OBJECTION #10

"I Only Buy American Products."

1. HOW ABOUT COLOMBIAN COFFEE, FRENCH WINES, AND JAPANESE TVs?

Do you use any of those products?

Chances are, you do.

<u>The point is, we live in a world economy.</u>

We all use products from different countries every day.

Why, all of a sudden, are you singling out our product, just because it is not made in America?

Is that fair??

Does that make sense??

2. **Do you feel that the U.S. government is anti-American?**

The government makes money on every single product we sell here— twice.

First on import duty and second on sales tax.

If it weren't profitable to the U.S. government, we wouldn't be allowed to sell these products here.

Our sales benefit every American!

3. Have you ever wondered why so many people wear sweaters made in Ireland, watches made in Switzerland, and cameras made in Japan? The reason is very simple.

They've got great products, and they've got great prices.

We are one of those companies with the best products and prices.

<u>It is really not important where our products are made.</u>

Doesn't it make sense to do business with us?

4. Did you know that any foreigner who has been in this country for a certain period of time can become a U.S. citizen?

Well, the same is true with our product. <u>We have been here so long, we are practically American.</u>

5. <u>Our company employs over 100 Americans.</u>
We pay thousands of dollars in taxes.
We're producing 20 percent of all the parts we use here in America.
Don't be fooled by our foreign-sounding name.
We are more American than most "American" companies!

6. You only buy American products??
That's almost impossible these days!

7. No one <u>only</u> buys American products.
It is impossible.
Since you obviously buy some foreign products, why are you suddenly discriminating against our company?
Is that fair??

8. You know, I am a very patriotic person too.

I BELIEVE IN SUPPORTING AMERICANS.

Did you know that over 2,000 Americans make their livings by working with our company?

How much more patriotic can you get??

9. <u>Did you hear about our new American manufacturing facility?</u>

That's right!

Starting in _____, we will be doing all of our manufacturing here in the U.S.A.

But, why wait??

Why not start benefiting from our high quality and low price <u>now</u>?

10. **No company in our industry makes all of its component parts in America.**

It is impossible to buy a "purely American" machine in this field.

Since that is true, why not focus on buying the <u>best value for the money?</u>

Doesn't that make sense?

11. WHO ARE YOU THINKING OF BUYING FROM?

Oh, _____ company.

Did you know that 90 percent of their parts are manufactured overseas?

They are as much a "foreign" company as we are.

Shouldn't you really concentrate on **the benefits** of the product rather than on whether it is made in one country or another??

12. Who are you thinking of buying from?

Oh, _____ company.

Please, do yourself a favor, and look beyond their American-sounding name.

They actually make more of their component parts overseas than we do.

If you are really pro-American, you will buy from us!

13. Did you know that we employ more American workers than 9 out of 10 of our competitors?

Isn't that important to you?

14. You only buy American?

Are you being straight with me?

Are you being completely honest with me??

15. What is more important, buying products from a certain country or getting the best value for your company?

Can I show you how to get the best value for your company?

16. You only buy American products?

I thought that was impossible in this day and age.

Could you explain what you mean by that?

17. Well, I am an American.
Why not buy from me??

18. _____
_____
_____

19. _____
_____
_____

OBJECTION #11

"We Tried Something Like It, but It Didn't Work."

1. What happened?

(Get **specific** information on the customer's complaints about the other product. Then show **specifically** how your product is different.)

2. Our product has been on the market for five years.

That other product was new and untested.

You won't have to worry about our product's reliability.

We guarantee it unconditionally!

3. (Prospect's name), have you ever eaten fast food that didn't agree with you?

One that gave you indigestion?

We all have.

Yet, you didn't give up eating just because that one meal upset you.

You said you've tried something that didn't work.

<u>I respect your experience, but please, do not compare our five-star meal with fast food!</u>

4. I'm sorry you had a bad experience.

I know how you feel.

I have disappointed myself with many purchases.

I can assure you that what we're offering is as different as night and day from that other product.

We guarantee it.

LET ME EXPLAIN EXACTLY HOW WE ARE DIFFERENT.

5. Let me show you these letters from satisfied customers.

See for yourself how we go about producing and backing up what we make.

<u>Did you ever see letters of praise like this for that other product?</u>

6. Was it really the product that didn't work or was it the service you didn't get?

We are known for having the best service in the industry.

Isn't that important to you?

7. That's unfortunate and I can understand how you feel.

Do you really think that this single experience will prevent you from looking at new and better opportunities?

8. **We have all been hurt at some time, haven't we?**

I am sure you have been hurt in love, right?

Has that turned you off to all relationships?

I hope not.

I respect the fact that you have been hurt.

I promise you that will not happen here.

We take outstanding care of our customers.

Can I tell you exactly how we do that?

9. Are we comparing apples with apples or apples with oranges?

Please do not compare us with that other company!

WE ARE TOTALLY DIFFERENT.

May I show you how we differ, and the many benefits we offer you?

10. Our product may look similar on the surface to _____'s product, but it <u>is only a superficial resemblance.</u>

I am sure you have heard that saying, "don't judge a book by its cover," right?

Well, it is really true in this case!

Can I open the book and show you the ways in which we are different and far superior??

11. **We are the Rolls Royce of the industry.**

IS IT REALLY FAIR TO COMPARE US TO A HYUNDAI?

Can I tell you more about what makes us the Rolls Royce?

12. How would you feel if your company's products were compared to the worst products in your industry??

Well, that is exactly the position you have just put me in.

<u>What would you do if you were in my position??</u>

May I please give you some information as to why we are far, far superior to that other company?

13. WHEN did you try it?

You know, great strides have been made in our industry since then!

The products we offer today are light years ahead of what you experienced back then!

Why not take a new look at what is available today?

14.

You know, comparing our products today with what that other company offered back then is like comparing a Model T with a Ferrari!

Is that really a fair comparison?

Don't you owe it to yourself to take a closer look at what is now available and how it can benefit your company??

15.

<u>You know, comparing our products today with what that other company offered back then is like comparing a 1990 computer with a 2006 computer.</u>

Today's computers are much more powerful, aren't they?

And, they cost less!

WE ARE IN EXACTLY THE SAME POSITION!

Our products are far superior to what you experienced in the past, and they cost less money!

Don't you owe it to your company to take a closer look at what today's technology offers?

16. _____
_____
_____

17. _____
_____
_____

OBJECTION #12

"Your Competitor's Product Is Better."

1. You're kidding?! (<u>Act surprised.</u>)

2. Better in what way?

    (<u>Have customer list features he/she likes in the other product; then show how yours has the same or better features.</u>)

3. I'd be interested in hearing your <u>unbiased</u> opinion on the two products.

4. Obviously, you've had a chance to look at their product.

    What did you see that impressed you?

5. Are you referring to quality, service, features, or the value of the product after five years of use?

6. Everyone has a unique way of presenting their product.

    <u>We</u> let the product speak for itself.

I'm positive that you will quickly see that there is a difference between promotional promises and actual facts.

Can I tell you what some of those differences are?

7. I would agree that there are some differences in design; however, what counts in the future is the quality of the service.

What advantage is there in having a slightly better figure on the spec sheet when you need same-day service—and they won't give it to you?

WE WILL GUARANTEE YOU SAME-DAY SERVICE.

How much is that worth to you??

8. With all the features you see in our competitor's product, there is one they can never have: our commitment to service.

We have more units in operation, more highly trained service engineers, and a better response record than anybody in the industry.

9. **I'm amazed that you would say that.**

We have a reputation as the best in the industry.

What, specifically, do you think is better in my competitor's product?

10. Our competitor's product appears to be better??

APPEARANCES CAN BE DECEIVING.

Let's take a look beneath the surface to see what you are really getting. Okay?

11. Who told you that?

Have you talked to people who own the two products, or have you only been listening to advertising??

I am sure that if you talk to owners, you will find that our product is far better respected than our competitor's.

12. SOME OF OUR HAPPIEST CUSTOMERS ARE PEOPLE WHO USED TO OWN THAT OTHER COMPANY'S PRODUCT!

Here, let me give you some phone numbers.

Call them up.

Let me tell you why our product is so far superior to the competition's product!

13. Better compared to what?

All of their major design features were "borrowed" from us.

That's merely a copycat product. (<u>State with disdain.</u>)

Our technology is two years ahead of theirs.

Shouldn't you take a closer look at what we are offering?

14.

It is true they may have some features we
don't have.

But please look at the price difference.

Their product costs much more up front
and their service calls are twice as expensive
as ours.

Over the course of five years, you could
pay twice as much for their product as
compared to ours.

And they both do the same job!

Why not do your company a favor and
save it some hard-earned money!

You don't need a gold-plated solution to
this problem.

Buy our product!

15. _____
_____

16. _____
_____
_____
_____

OBJECTION #13

"We Expect Hard Times Ahead."

1. That's exactly the reason why we recommend buying now, so that you will be able to <u>meet the hard times head-on with increased productivity.</u>

2. **If you were the captain of an ocean liner, you wouldn't stop sailing just because you saw a little storm cloud on the horizon, would you?**

Well, your company is like that ocean liner.

Are you going to stop leading and managing your company just because there might be some difficult times ahead?

3. You know what they say about the success rate of economic forecasters?

They accurately predicted nine of the last two recessions.

(<u>Say this with a smile in your voice.</u>)

Are you absolutely sure a depression is ahead?

Even if there is, it may be smart to do what many of our clients do and give us a large order now to have materials on hand if times get tough.

4. **Hard times call for a harder look at lower costs and higher profits.**

Luckily, you'll get both with our product. Why not place an order today?

5. **Is it just a matter of money?**

If so, I am certain we will be able to extend you credit to pay this off conveniently.

Shall we look at our credit terms?

6. Why do you expect hard times ahead?

7. **Who told you** there will be hard times ahead?

Does he really have a crystal ball?

Can anyone really predict the future??

8.
How did you get so scared about the future?

9.
That surprises me.

<u>Most of the people in your industry are expecting good times ahead.</u>

Do you think they could all be that wrong??

10.
How far ahead?

Sure, maybe in a year or two—but that is a long way off.

WHY START PULLING BACK NOW??

Everyone is predicting that <u>the next couple of quarters will be excellent.</u>

Why not take advantage of that good business today?

11.
You know, Dr. Norman Vincent Peale was once interviewed in *Selling Power* and he said that researchers have found that <u>98 percent of all the things we worry about never come true!</u>

Could this be one of those things?

What if you worry about it, cut back, and it never comes true?

Do you want to take that risk??

12. Well, if you are expecting hard times ahead, maybe you should just <u>cut back a little on your order.</u>

I am not suggesting you buy a warehouse full!

But, does it make any sense to do without completely??

13. You know, when times were tough in the Depression, people had to do with less food.

They had to cut back.

But, those people who cut back too much, they starved and died.

The same thing can happen to businesses!

<u>Don't starve your business.</u>

<u>It is not healthy!</u>

Shouldn't we place a small order today?

14. What do you think the biggest businesses in your industry will be doing?

Are they going to cut back and lose market share?

NO!

Why not do what the big boys do?

This could be an excellent opportunity to take business away from the smaller and weaker companies in your field.

Why not place an order today?

15. _____
_____
_____

16. _____
_____
_____

OBJECTION #14

"Your Product Is Too New."

_1._   **How new is new?**

Our product has been on the market for several years!

_2._   Are you saying that it is not safe to use?

Would you like to see what the top safety experts have said about our product?

_3._   I DID NOT WANT YOU TO GET THE IMPRESSION THAT WE ARE USING OUR CUSTOMERS AS A TESTING LABORATORY.

You may be one of the first in this area to use this product; however, it has been tried and tested for more than two years all over the U.S.A.

It is only new around here.

_4._   It's not altogether new since all the basic elements from our previous model are the same.

There are over 60 percent interchangeable parts between the two models.

And, as you know, our last model was considered the workhorse and the standard of the industry!

We are certain this product will be even more highly respected!

5. **That's exactly the reason why you should get one.**

You're a smart businessperson and you know you're getting a great deal on our introductory offer.

If you buy two months from now, you'll have to pay 10 percent more.

WHY NOT BUY TODAY AND TAKE ADVANTAGE OF THE SAVINGS?

6. Let me show you a few letters from customers who have bought this excellent product a few months ago.

They haven't had any problems.

They're very happy.

7. I believe that our company puts out the best product line in the industry.

    This latest model was put together using the precise quality standards we've established from being in business over 20 years.

    You won't have to worry about quality, service, or reliability.

8. **You know, everything was new at one time.**

    At one time, the telephone was new, the computer was new, the automobile was new.

    <u>Some businesses took advantage of these new inventions and tools, and most of these businesses prospered.</u>

    Other businesses clung to old technology and outdated tools, and most of those businesses failed.

    <u>Aren't we in the same situation here today?</u>

    Why not be one of the forward-looking businesses?

Take advantage of this new opportunity for productivity before your competitors do. Can we place your order today?

9. Is it really fair to discriminate against a company or a product just because it is new?

At one time your company was new, and it introduced new products.

How would you have felt if no one had looked at your products just because they were new?

Won't you please show me the courtesy of at least looking at the benefits of our new products?

10. **Someday, this product will be old and outdated.**

Obviously, you don't want to wait until then to buy it, do you?

Well, when would you like to buy it?

Why not place an order now, for delivery in three months?

If you hear anything at all bad about our product in the next three months, we won't ship it. Okay?

By then, it won't be brand new.

But, by buying today, you will be able to take advantage of the special introductory price we have.

So, you are a winner all the way around.

Can we place your order today?

11. Has your company ever, ever bought a new product you liked?

When?

Why?

Aren't we in a similar situation here today?

I am sure that if you buy this new product, you will love it.

12. **Does your company buy used cars for its people?**

No?

Then why should it buy used or outdated technology?

That doesn't make sense, does it?

13. <u>Do you know why we were losing our competitive edge to the Japanese?</u>

It was because we did not keep up with technology.

We did not keep up with modern manufacturing methods.

Buying this new machine will not only be good for you, it will be good for America.

Can we place your order today?

14. _____

_____

_____

15. _____

_____

_____

OBJECTION #15

"Business Is Slow Right Now."

1. <u>I'm sure that you have plans for improving this situation.</u>

Our system can help you.

Can I show you how we can help you improve business?

2. Is this slump going to last forever?

No.

Then **now** is the best time to sit down and discuss what you'll need when this temporary slowdown ends and your business picks up.

3. What are the consequences of this?

4. I understand.

<u>Since business is slow right now, that means that you should be especially interested in finding ways to save money on operation costs.</u>

Correct?

Then, you need my product now more than ever!

5. Business is slow?

Then I'm glad I came <u>today</u>.

Let's talk about how we can help you make money.

6. If business is slow, you need to improve productivity fast.

I'VE WORKED WITH MANY PEOPLE IN SIMILAR SITUATIONS.

Would you like to hear what our machinery helped them accomplish?

7. Here is a list of customers who bought from us to increase their business volume.

Some of them have been able to bring in so much new business, they actually work overtime right now.

8. **How slow is slow?**

Exactly how much has it slowed down?

If it increases 10 percent next month, will you buy from us?

Do you promise?

9. Has it ever been slow in the past?

What did you do then?

Did you cut back on all of your purchases? Of course not.

But, I respect that you do have to prioritize purchases.

Let me give you some good reasons why our product should be at the top of your priority list.

10. WHAT DO YOU THINK THE REALLY BIG COMPANIES IN YOUR FIELD DO WHEN BUSINESS SLOWS DOWN A LITTLE?

Do you think they completely cut off all purchases and board up the windows?

OBJECTION # 15

Of course not.

I respect your need to prioritize purchase decisions.

But I suggest you think like the big boys.

Cut back on your purchases, but still make the vital purchases.

Let me show you why our equipment is so essential to you now.

11. You remind me of Mr. _____ in _____.

His business slowed down a little and he cut way back.

He cut back on almost all important purchases.

WHEN BUSINESS PICKED UP AGAIN, HE WASN'T READY.

He couldn't handle it.

HE LOST HIS BUSINESS TO HIS COMPETITORS.

I'd hate to see anything like this happen to you.

Why not buy this machine so that you will be ready for the upturn in business?

12. Business is slow right now?

<u>Then, this is the perfect time to buy!</u>

When business is booming, your people won't have the time to learn how to operate a new machine.

Now while times are temporarily slow is the perfect time to get this new machine in.

When business picks up, they will all be skilled on the machine.

Can we place your order today?

13. _____

_____

_____

14. _____

_____

_____

OBJECTION #16

"I'm Not Interested."

1.

There is no reason on Earth why you should be interested in our product until I can show you how it can help you make money, increase productivity, and solve some of your problems.

CAN I SHOW YOU HOW WE CAN ACCOMPLISH THAT?

2.

(Prospect's name), 70 business executives have bought this product over the last two weeks and they all began by saying they were not interested.

They only bought because they found it would save them money and cut down on their headaches.

Would you like to learn what they learned?

3.

May I ask you to consider your company's interests for a moment?

I believe that my product will help you produce extra cash.

OBJECTION # 16

I would appreciate your looking at the evidence, and then I'll leave it to your judgment, of course, to decide whether or not you want it.

4. **May I ask why?**

5. This is a calculated call.

　We just installed a system in a company like yours.

　They are now saving money and sleeping better at night.

　Isn't your main interest in saving money?

　Can I show you how we help companies save money?

6. I would be interested in your reasons why.

　Did I say something that offended you?

7. You are not interested in making money???

8.
You are not interested??

We very rarely hear that!

Could you explain to me how you could not be interested in saving money and making money?

I thought that was why you were in business.

9.
I wouldn't be interested if I were you, either.

You don't have the latest information.

Can I tell you something about our products so that you can decide if they are truly of interest to your company or not?

10.
You know, at some point, you weren't interested in buying a new car.

At some point, you weren't interested in buying a new house.

But, as you learned more about cars and houses, your interest level rose, and when the time was right for you, you bought.

I am not asking you to buy today.

I am only asking you to listen to a proposal that may benefit you greatly.

May I explain to you some of the many benefits of your products?

11. A lot of people say that just to get off the phone.

Am I calling you at a bad time?

If so, I would be happy to call you at a more convenient time.

I know <u>YOU WILL BE INTERESTED</u> when you hear what we have been able to accomplish for our client companies.

It is very exciting!

When would be a better time to talk?

12. You are not interested?

<u>Then who should I talk to in your company</u> who would be interested in saving money and increasing productivity?

13. **You are not interested now, or forever?**

Should I call back next month when things are less hectic?

14. You are not interested?

I apologize to you.

I know I must have done something wrong.

If I had fully explained the many benefits of our product, I know you would be interested.

You'd be very excited.

What did I neglect to explain to you?

15. _____

_____

_____

16. _____

_____

_____

OBJECTION #17

"I'm Sorry; We Won't Buy from You."

1. **Why??**

2. Obviously, you must have a reason for feeling that way.

   May I ask what it is?

3. I am sure you've considered the pros and cons before you made this decision.

   I'd be interested to know what items tilted the balance.

4. Can you do me a favor?

   Could you get me some aspirin?

   Where did I go wrong? (Humorously.)

5. Are you saying that you no longer need to cut your costs or improve productivity?

6. Don't be sorry.

   We have more business than we can handle right now.

   However, I'd be curious to know what exactly changed your mind.

7.

Who did you decide to buy from?

Well, that is a good company, but IF YOU EVER WANT SOME BACKUP, IF YOU DON'T WANT TO PUT ALL YOUR EGGS IN ONE BASKET, you might consider buying some of that product from us.

It could be a good insurance policy for you, just in case.

8.

You are buying from someone else?

That is surprising.

I thought we had the order last week.

What happened?

9.

You are buying from someone else?

Has the purchase order been signed?

Have you paid them yet?

You know, you can still change your mind.

Many people do, and no one takes it personally.

Let me review for you the many benefits of our product.

You may want to get out of that other order before it is too late.

10. You won't buy from us??

Is it just a matter of price?

If that is all it is, I am sure I can have some easy-to-pay credit terms extended to you.

Shall I call our credit manager now?

11. Are you not going to buy from us now, or forever??

What could we do to win your business in the future??

12. I respect the fact that you aren't buying from us now.

However, you did say that you liked our product very much.

Do you know anyone else in the business who might be interested in our products?

Who?

13. Is there anyone else in your company who might be interested in buying our cost-saving products?

Who?

14. I respect the fact that you aren't buying from us this one time.

<u>However, I suspect that as you hear more and more about our fantastic products in the news and from customers, you will buy something from us in the future.</u>

Do you mind if I stop by periodically to keep you up-to-date on our new products?

Great!

I will look forward to seeing you next month!

15. _____

_____

_____

16. _____

_____

_____

OBJECTION #18

"The Machine We Have Is Still Good."

1. I understand how you feel.

Many of my customers have said that before they switched over.

However, they found that the reason a new model makes an old model obsolete is not that the old one is bad, but that the new one is so much more efficient and productive.

Would you like to take a look at what these progressive businesses found?

2. That's exactly why you should trade now.

Since your machine is still good, you still have a high trade-in value.

When it breaks down, your trade-in value will go down too.

It's actually less expensive to trade in a workable machine than to wait for it to fail.

Can we write your order up today?

3. Have you ever figured the useful economic life of your machine?

The downtime, the repair cost, the slower operation, the limits of its availability?

I agree, your old machine still runs, but it also runs up some high maintenance bills.

WOULDN'T IT BE NICE TO GET RID OF ALL THOSE MAINTENANCE BILLS?

Our new machine comes with a full warranty!

4. BEING GOOD MAY NOT BE GOOD ENOUGH IN TODAY'S ECONOMY.

Look at what your competitors are doing.

They are always trying to be better, to use the benefits of the latest technology.

Why not try to be the best?

Be a leader instead of a follower.

5. The longer you keep this machine, the older it will get and the more costly it will become for you to upgrade.

Not to mention safety risks.

Do you really want to worry about the safety of your workers who use this machine??

6. Good compared to what?
What standards are you using?

7. **What do your customers think when they see this old machine you have?**
Do you think that impresses them?
Wouldn't you like to have a machine in here that really impresses your customers and inspires their trust?

8. It still looks good on the surface.
But, as we both know, appearances can be deceptive.
Chances are, it has a number of weak and worn parts internally.
Do you really want to take the chance of having it break down someday when you really need it?

9. Have you fallen in love with this machine?

While this old machine still works, it is not nearly as functional or productive as it could be.

Buy one of our new machines and I guarantee <u>you will love it</u> even more than this old one!

10.

<u>What stops you from buying a new machine?</u>
<u>Is it only the price?</u>

If so, I am sure we can arrange easy credit terms with our finance people.

Shall I call them now?

11.

THINK OF YOUR TOUGHEST COMPETITORS.

DO THEY WAIT UNTIL A MACHINE IS COMPLETELY BROKEN DOWN BEFORE THEY REPLACE IT?

I doubt it!

<u>One of the things that makes them so successful is that they look to the future.</u>

They are prepared for the future!

Why not think like an industry leader!

If you think and act like an industry leader, it can only add to your success!

12. You know, outdoor plumbing still works.

ROTARY TELEPHONES STILL WORK.

But, when a better way comes along, most people use it.

Why are you resisting the technology that is now available??

13. What kind of car do you drive?

Oh, that is a nice car!

How old is it?

Good, it is a new car!

You are a person who appreciates quality and reliability.

Why are you holding back now?

Why are you denying yourself and your company?

Does that make sense?

14. **Are you afraid your people won't be able to use this new machine?**

Let me assure you, we have the best training program in the industry!

<u>In a very short period of time, your people will find this new machine even easier to operate than that old one!</u>

Shall we place your order today?

15. _____
_____
_____

16. _____
_____
_____

OBJECTION #19

"We Are Satisfied with What We Have Now."

1.   Satisfied in what way?

2.   I am pleased that you're satisfied.

     That's a good position to be in.

     <u>However, I think that you'd be even more satisfied by the many unique benefits of our product.</u>

     May I tell you about its features and benefits?

3.   I know how you feel.

     Often we're satisfied with a product or service because we have no chance to compare it with something better.

     May I show you the top reference standard in the industry?

4.   **As a manager, I am certain that you remind your employees not to be satisfied with their results, but to strive to improve them.**

Your business depends upon improvement.

I wouldn't be here today if I weren't convinced that I can help improve your situation. Can I show you how?

5. <u>Most people are satisfied with what they have.</u>

Most of our current customers were happy with what they had, before they saw our product.

There are three reasons they switched.

<u>(State three product benefits.)</u>

6. What do you like most about what you have right now?

<u>(Then show them how your product has even more of this.)</u>

7. **I am glad to hear that.**

I wouldn't want to talk with you if you weren't.

We like to deal with people who make good purchase decisions.

Smart people really appreciate what we have to offer.

May I tell you about our special product?

8. **What did you have before you bought what you have now?**

WHY DID YOU SWITCH??

Obviously, you had some good reasons for changing.

It may be time to change again.

Let me show you why more and more intelligent consumers are switching to our product.

9. I know what you are saying.

You don't like to change without good reasons, correct?

I understand and respect that.

Let me give you some solid reasons why more and more purchasing managers are switching to our products.

10. You don't know what satisfaction is until you use our service!

11. **No company is perfect, not even ours.**

If you could change anything at all about the company you are doing business with or their product, what would it be?

(Now, show them how they can get this with your company.)

12. Have you always been satisfied?

Have they ever let you down?

You know, we have the best service in the industry.

We guarantee same-day service.

No other company does that.

Don't you think that would make you even more satisfied??

13.

You hate change, don't you?

I am the same way.

But, sometimes you just have to change to keep up with the competition.

<u>Can I show you how changing to our products will help you get ahead of your competitors?</u>

14.

Did you read *In Search of Excellence*?

You know, that book sold more than five million copies.

The main idea is that excellent companies are not content to merely be satisfied with things the way they are.

They constantly look for ways of improving.

<u>They strive to be the best.</u>

Isn't that how you are?

<u>Can I show you how our products can help your company join the ranks of truly excellent corporations?</u>

15. _____

_____

_____

16. _____

_____

_____

OBJECTION #20

"I Have to Think This Over."

1. What **exactly** do you want to think about?

2. Let's think it over out loud.
   Sometimes two heads are better than one.
   Is it the financing you're concerned about, or is it something about the design you'd like to think over?

3. Let's think about it now while it is fresh in your mind.
   WHAT ARE SOME OF THE ITEMS YOU NEED TO KNOW MORE ABOUT?

4. You have made bigger decisions than this before, haven't you?
   WHY NOT SAVE TIME AND GET THIS ONE OUT OF YOUR WAY?

5. As busy as you are, you probably have other things to think about that are more important.
   I imagine this is a relatively small decision for a person like you.

WHY NOT MAKE THE DECISION RIGHT NOW AND FREE YOUR MIND TO THINK ABOUT THE REALLY BIG ISSUES IN YOUR BUSINESS?

Okay?

6. **You impress me as a proactive decision maker.**

Why don't we take the bull by the horns on this one and make a decision now?

7. Fine, I will wait out in the lobby, and you can come out when you have made up your mind. (<u>Humorously.</u>)

8. Obviously, you must have a reason for saying that.

Would you mind if I ask what it is?

9. I understand that you want more time to think.

<u>I would be interested in your thoughts about the reasons for and the reasons against buying now.</u>

10.

You should think it over, (<u>Prospect's name</u>).

Any time you can save money, you should give it a great deal of thought.

But, you know, there are a great many things we can think about and always come up with the same answer.

For example, if I asked you the color of your car, whether you think it over for 10 minutes, 10 days, or 10 weeks, you'll always come up with the same answer.

In the same way, you can think about this proposal for 10 minutes, 10 days, or even 10 weeks.

You'll always come to the same conclusion: that it's never a mistake to save money.

Can't we make the decision to buy today?

11. <u>Thinking this over could mean that you'll have to wait two months before you can enjoy the benefits of our product.</u>

We can condense these two months to two minutes if you will accept my proposal now.

Can we go ahead?

12. Why invest more time thinking this over?

You've told me you have already invested dozens of hours in thinking about this.

Haven't you thought about it enough?

13. I know what you're saying, yet I sense you'd like to get this unfinished business over with.

I also feel that there are some points that you really like.

<u>What is it that's holding you back?</u>

14. Don't think about it too long!

You know our price is scheduled to go up next month.

Can't we take advantage of today's low price and order now?

15. Don't think about it too long!
Your time is valuable!
Don't spend $500 of your time thinking about a decision this small.
Can't we go ahead today?

16. You want to think about it?
Great!
Why don't you think about it intensively for three hours, and I will call you this afternoon. Okay?

17. You want to think about it?
I know what you are really saying.
You are saying I didn't make the benefits of owning our product clear to you.
If I had made those benefits clear, I know you'd be ready to buy now.

I apologize for that.

Now, what didn't I make clear to you?

18. You and I have been thinking this over since the time we first met.

You know that this is a terrific opportunity, you like the product, and you know it will save you money.

Let's go ahead now.

19. _____

_____

_____

20. _____

_____

_____

OBJECTION #21

"I Need to Talk to My Boss About It."

1. If it's a question of selling him/her on the idea of buying, I'd suggest that we go together so I can help you with any of his questions.

2. Of course you do.

WHAT ARE SOME OF THE IDEAS YOU WILL BE DISCUSSING WITH HER/HIM?

3. **I can save you time.**

Let's see him/her now so we can wrap this up and you'll be able to begin enjoying the benefits of this product even sooner!

4. **It might take you some time to learn my presentation.**

I can save you time, and I am paid to do this.

All you need to do is introduce us and I'll do the rest.

Let's set up a time for me and her/him to get together.

5. <u>What would happen if you took the bull by the horns and made the decision now?</u>

I really think your boss will congratulate you for showing initiative and good judgment.

6. **Are you sure you want to bother your boss with such a small expense?**

Can't you really make this decision yourself?

7. Does your boss get involved in every purchase decision?

<u>When has she/he not been involved?</u>

Do you think this might be another time not to trouble her/him?

8. **You know, I wouldn't try to do your job, and you don't have to try to do my job.**

Why not just set up a time for me to talk to him/her?

9. **How long did it take you to learn your job?**

Well, it took me about two years to learn my job.

I wouldn't try to do your job, and you don't have to do mine.

Give me your boss' phone number, and I will be happy to see him/her.

What is his number? _____

10. **You know, our product is very complicated, isn't it?**

I wouldn't expect you to memorize all the details, facts, features, and benefits of our products.

That would be overwhelming.

Why not just let me go in and give it all to her/him directly?

11. **Why** do you need to talk with him/her?

12. Why don't you go talk to her/him now.

I will wait here.

If he/she has any questions, I will be happy to answer them.

13. **When** will you talk with him/her?

Good!

I will call you tomorrow afternoon and find out if we can go ahead!

14. **Have you ever surprised your wife (husband) with a present?**

<u>Well, maybe it is time to surprise your boss!</u>

Think of how happy she/he will be when you tell her/him you have bought this fantastic machine that will help your company make so much money!

Can we place the order today?

15. _____

_____

_____

16. _____

_____

_____

OBJECTION #22

"I Can't Afford It."

1.

I would agree if we were talking about luxuries.

But, you and I are talking about <u>necessities.</u>

Wouldn't you agree that for a business such as yours, it is necessary to cut costs and improve productivity?

How can you not afford it?

2.

(<u>Prospect's name</u>), all of us have just so much money we can use for buying things. Correct?

So, it isn't a question of being able to "afford" this product, but one of using some funds in a different way.

Let's talk this over and see if we can find a way to meet this challenge.

<u>I know you don't have an unlimited budget.</u>

Let me show you how inexpensive it really is to own one of these.

3. That reminds me of the old saying, "We all buy things we can't afford to impress people we don't like."

    But, we're not talking about impressing people here, we're talking about improving their productivity.

    <u>What could be more important than that?</u>

4. I SINCERELY BELIEVE THAT YOU CANNOT AFFORD NOT TO BUY THIS.

    The benefits of lower costs, faster operation, better service, and superior quality far outweigh the price.

5. Obviously you must have a reason for saying that.

    Do you mind if I ask what it is?

6. If I could show you a way you can afford this purchase, would you be interested?

7. Is it just a matter of money?

If you could afford it, would you want it?

Great!

Let me call our credit department now.

I am sure we can work out an easy payment plan to get you this machine!

8. I know what you are really telling me.

<u>What you are really saying is that this is not a top priority for you.</u>

I know that we all find the money for the things that are really important, don't we?

Let me explain to you how the many benefits of this product should make it a top priority for you.

9. **What are you spending your money on?**

What could be more important than this?

OBJECTION # 22

10. **Are you telling me that you don't have money in your budget for this?**

I understand.

I know how corporate budgets operate.

But, let me tell you that <u>we have been paid out of many different budgets.</u>

While you may not have money in one budget area for us, I am certain you do in another area.

Let's take a closer look at your budget. Okay?

11. Do you mean you can't afford it now, or forever?

Why not reserve a unit NOW at today's low prices.

We can delay shipment until the next quarter when you will have more money.

Okay?

12. You cannot afford to be without it!

There is a price to pay for having the machine and there is a price to pay for not having it.

THE COST OF NOT HAVING IT IS GREATER THAN THE COST OF HAVING IT.

Think of all the business you can lose, the productivity you can lose, the lost income from not having the latest, best, and most reliable technology.

Do you really want to pay that price?

13. You can't afford it??

Is this a temporary condition or a permanent condition?

Good, it is temporary!

WHEN SHOULD I CALL ON YOU AGAIN?

OBJECTION # 22

14. _____
_____
_____

15. _____
_____
_____

OBJECTION #23

"I'll Buy a Used One."

OBJECTION
23

1. <u>I don't need to tell you that it will cost you more in the long run!</u>

2. **When you buy a used product, you're really taking a high risk.**

You buy something that someone else has used and possibly abused.

DO YOU WANT TO PAY FOR OTHER PEOPLE'S MISTAKES?

3. You may save a few dollars on your monthly payments, but you'll have to pay much more in extra service, more repairs, and downtime.

Which price would you rather pay?

4. <u>Many of our customers thought about getting a used product before they decided to get a new one.</u>

Let me show you why they decided that new equipment is the best buy.

The cost comparisons will make it all clear.

5. **I understand you want to save money.**

I like to save money.

But, you have to draw the line somewhere. <u>Buying a used product in this field is like shopping for a headache.</u>

PERHAPS YOU SHOULD CONSIDER THE SMALLER MODEL FOR STARTERS.

At least you won't have any worries about its reliability!

6. **Do you really want to do this to yourself?**

Do you really want to give up a full-factory warranty, an excellent performance guarantee, and superior quality?

Is it worth losing all that to have a few extra bucks in your pocket?

7. Did you ever buy anything used that was any good?

That didn't cost you an arm and a leg to keep running?

No.

Why do you think this will be any different?

8. **Do you buy used clothing?**

No.

Why not? You could save money on it!

Well, we are in a similar situation here.

You might save a few dollars by buying used merchandise.

But please think about your pride and self-respect.

Don't you really deserve new merchandise?

9. **What kind of people buy new things?**

Winners.

Don't you want to be a winner?

I THINK YOU ARE A WINNER.

You impress me as a person on the way up.

Why not buy a NEW model?

Don't you deserve the best?

10. You will buy a used product???

You are kidding me, aren't you?

11. **Have you ever bought a used machine <u>of this type</u> before?**

Well, many of our customers have.

Let me tell you what they learned.

<u>Used machinery may be a good buy in some fields, but it definitely isn't in this field!</u>

I've never met anyone who bought a used machine who was truly happy with it.

Learn and benefit from their experience.

Don't make that mistake.

Buy a new machine!

12. **Where will you find a used machine like this?**

They very rarely come on the market.

When it does, it is usually a beaten-up, broken-down model.

Instead of waiting months to find a used machine, which will probably not be in very good shape, doesn't it make more sense to buy a new machine today?

13. **Do you think a used machine will be <u>safe</u> for your workers?**

Do you think you will be able to get a full service record with it?

Probably not.

Are you going to be able to sleep at night knowing that your workers may be operating dangerous machinery?

Doesn't it make more sense to get some reliable, **safe** new machinery?

14. You are going to buy a used machine?

Is it only a matter of money?

If so, let me call our credit department today.

I am sure we can arrange easy payment terms to get you the new machine you really want.

THE MONTHLY PAYMENTS WILL BE AS LOW AS FOR A USED MACHINE!

Shall I call our credit department now?

15. _____

_____

_____

16. _____

_____

_____

OBJECTION #24

"I Want to Get a Couple Prices First."

1. <u>I understand that you need a price and I'd like to help you out.</u>

    What, specifically, are you looking for?

    You see, shopping for a product like the one you're considering is like shopping for transportation: You can buy a car or a jet, or you could get a bicycle.

    What, exactly, do you want?

2. Of course you do.

    <u>I encourage you to look around before you make the final decision.</u>

    Let me ask you a question.

    What other brands have you considered that might be able to suit your needs?

    Let's compare features and benefits.

3. Great.

    I'm glad you told me that.

    I have the price lists of our major competitors right here.

    Let's save time and go over them now.

4. **Will you be the only one evaluating features and prices, or will someone else be involved?** (Wait for an answer.)

   If your partner will be in on this decision, I owe it to both of you to explain to him/her the many unique features and benefits of our product.

   What is your partner's phone number?
   I will call him/her today.

5. Obviously, you must have a reason for getting more prices.

   Do you mind if I ask what it is?

6. **Is price the most important criterion to you?**

   If you are only looking for a cheap product, I can tell you right now who has the cheapest product.

   They also have the worst warranty and the lowest quality.

<u>Aren't you really interested in value for the dollar?</u>

Can I show you why we are the best value?

7. You want to get a couple of additional prices? Good!

I will call you back tomorrow and we will discuss what you found out. Okay?

Happy hunting!

8. You want to get a few more prices?

You've already told me that you've spent two weeks looking at products in this field.

<u>Your time is valuable, isn't it?</u>

How much more of your valuable time will you spend on getting product information and prices?

Don't you really have enough information to make this decision today?

9. You want to get more prices?

Why all the time and energy spent on this?

You make bigger decisions than this every day, don't you?

Why not just take the bull by the horns and make a decision now, okay?

10. **Is it only a matter of money?**

If so, let me call our credit department today.

I am sure we can arrange a payment schedule that will be easy for you to live with.

11. _____
_____
_____

12. _____
_____
_____

OBJECTION #25

"I Have to Receive Two More Estimates."

1. I understand that you want to compare the prices and values that each product has to offer.

I encourage my clients to do so.

Let me ask you a question.

BASED ON WHAT I'VE SHOWN YOU TODAY, WHAT ARE SOME OF THE REASONS FOR AND AGAINST GOING WITH US?

2. **I don't blame you for shopping around.**

I was wondering: What criteria have you set for comparing these estimates?

What key requirements are you looking for?

3. **You impress me as a very busy person.**

I'd like to save you some time.

I have the prices of our competitors here in my briefcase.

We can go over them now and make a decision.

4. If you look very hard, you might find someone who, at first glance, would seem less expensive.

But, they will have to cut corners somewhere.

<u>It may be on the quality, or they may cut corners on your service.</u>

Are you willing to accept these cuts, or would you like to save money by getting the best quality and the best service?

5. I am glad you brought that up.

When you compare prices and value, the logical choice is our company.

I have studied the prices of other companies for years and I haven't found one that can give you better quality and better service, at a better price.

6. THERE ARE THREE POSSIBILITIES WITH GETTING MORE ESTIMATES.

One, you could go through all this work and find out that we're lower. (Pause.)

Would you buy if we were lowest?

The second possibility would be that we're all equally priced.

Would you buy from us then?

That leaves the third possibility that we would be higher.

In that case, you and I can discuss what item to cut out of our proposal to save you money.

No matter what you find out from the other estimates, we need to talk.

Will you call me as soon as you get those estimates.

7.

You know, I have been offered jobs by many companies in this industry.

I want to tell you something about myself.

I am basically a lazy man.

I LIKE TO SELL THE BEST PRODUCT AVAILABLE, AT THE BEST PRICE.

That is why I am still with this company.

No one else has a product that can match ours for price and quality.

Why don't you benefit from all my years of research and go with our company?

I guarantee—you won't be able to find a better deal!

8. **Please, go ahead and do your research and get your estimates.**

After you have gotten all your estimates, come back to me.

If you can find a deal that beats ours—and I don't think you will be able to—**I will match it!**

9. Many of our customers have received estimates from all over town.

Here, I have copies in my briefcase.

Let's look at their estimates.

You will see that no company can offer you what we offer!

All the homework has been done for you!

Can't you make your decision now?

10.

Who said you have to receive two more estimates?

Does your boss want you to?

Does your spouse want you to?

No?

<u>Don't you have better things to do with your time than run around looking for more estimates?</u>

Why not make a positive decision now?

11.

This is pocket change for someone like you, isn't it?

Why waste so much time on such a small decision?

Can't you decide today with all the information you have?

12. **What would happen if you didn't get the estimates?**

Would the world come to an end?

Of course not!

You have made bigger decisions than this without lots of estimates.

LET'S MAKE THE DECISION NOW AND GET THIS CLEARED OFF YOUR DESK.

Can we write the order up now?

13. _____

_____

_____

14. _____

_____

_____

OBJECTION #26

"I Don't Have Any Money for This."

1. I know how you feel.

Usually when we say that we don't have the money, we really mean that we want to hold back until that exceptional opportunity comes along.

Right?

Let me tell you, this is one of those exceptional opportunities.

2. I respect that.

I didn't think you had the budget of Microsoft.

If I could show you two ways where the product will really pay for itself, would you be interested?

3. Are you aware <u>how little it costs per month</u> to own one of these?

4. **You don't have to give us <u>your</u> money.**

If fact, <u>we can give you the money</u> so you can own this product.

Let's look at the finance plan.

5. **This product won't cost you money; it will make you money.**

The question of money boils down to how much you can put aside from your future profits.

6. That's exactly why you should buy now.

This product is designed for people with no money.

This will help you create more money.

7. You know the old saying. **"Money attracts money."**

We can say today, "Our product attracts money."

IT IS LIKE HAVING A MONEY-MAKING MACHINE.

Every hour of operation will put $45 cash in your pocket.

How can you afford to be without it?

Can we fill out the paperwork today?

8. You don't have any money?

No money at all?

Oh, you do have some money . . .

9. **What are you spending all that money on?**

Let me show you how our machine (<u>or service</u>) can <u>save you money</u>.

WHEN I COME IN HERE THREE MONTHS FROM NOW, I WANT YOU TO SAY, "I'VE GOT LOTS OF MONEY!"

And, I know our machine will help put you in that position.

Can I show you how?

10. Well, **you** may not have any money.

But, **does anyone else in this company have a budget** to buy some much needed machinery?

WHO? _____ WHAT IS HIS NUMBER? _____

Good! I will talk with him today!

11. You don't have any money **now—or forever?**

Good! YOU WILL HAVE SOME MONEY IN THE FUTURE!

When do you think you will have this money?

Great, <u>I will call you a few weeks before then</u> and we will get you enjoying our product as soon as possible!

12. What did you spend all your money on?

Did you know you could sell some of this old machinery and have enough money to buy a new machine?

IT IS EASY!

Let me show you how it's done!

13. **If you did have the money, would you want it?**

Good!

<u>Since you do want it</u>, let me show you how we can help you afford it!

14. If you do <u>find you have some money</u> somewhere in your budget, do you promise you will call me?

Great!

Here is my phone number.

I hope to hear from you!

15. _____
_____
_____

16. _____
_____
_____

OBJECTION #27

"Why Should I Buy from You When I Can Get a Similar Product for Much Less?"

1.   <u>Would you want to have a lawyer represent you who charged much less per hour?</u>

One, let's say, who charges you $15 instead of $100?

Wouldn't you be a little concerned about how much he/she is really going to cost you at judgment time?

2.   If our competitor is much less, what does that tell you?

Maybe they really know how much their product is worth.

3.   I am glad you brought that up, because many of my current customers made similar comments before buying from us.

THEY'VE FOUND THAT OUR PRICE IS HIGHER, YET IT IS A GREAT VALUE.

<u>Let me give you the names and phone numbers of some of our customers.</u>

Let them tell you in their own words why we are worth much more than we charge!

4. Sure you can get any product for much less.

You can get an imitation Rolex for less than $50.

The question is: Are you going to be happy with a look-alike when you can have an original?

5. **When you go in for medical treatment, do you just look for the cheapest price?**

Of course not!

Wouldn't you be suspicious of a doctor who only charged $15 an hour?

ISN'T THIS PURCHASE JUST AS IMPORTANT AS MEDICAL CARE?

After all, it will have a direct bearing on the health of your company!

Buy from us and make your company even healthier!

6. **Are you the cheapest in your industry?**
No?

Well, what do you say when people tell you they can get your products for less?

Aren't we in a similar situation here today?

YOU AND I ARE ALIKE.

WE DON'T DO THINGS THE CHEAP WAY.

WE BELIEVE IN QUALITY!

Shouldn't you really be doing business with us?

7. What kind of car do you drive?

Oh. That is a nice car.

<u>You are obviously a person who appreciates quality!</u>

You didn't get cheap when it came to your car.

Why are you cutting corners now??

That isn't like you, is it?

Shouldn't you buy our high-quality product?

8. The other product may look similar, but it definitely is not!

You and I both know, **appearances can be deceptive!**

You have heard the saying, "DON'T JUDGE A BOOK BY ITS COVER!"

Let me show you why our product is so vastly superior!

9. YOU KNOW, CHEAP WINE LOOKS VERY SIMILAR TO EXPENSIVE WINE.

However, there is a world of difference!

It is the same with our products.

WHILE OTHERS MAY SUPERFICIALLY LOOK SIMILAR, THEY ARE AS DIFFERENT AS NIGHT AND DAY!

Let me show you why we are the industry leaders in quality and reliability!

10. While the product may look similar, **the service contract and warranty are completely different!**

We offer a <u>full</u> guarantee and same-day service.

You will have virtually no downtime with our machine.

How much is that worth to you?

11. What neighborhood do you live in?

<u>Gee, that is a beautiful neighborhood!</u>

You didn't cut corners when it came time for buying a house.

Why cut corners now?

Isn't it true that you are a person who appreciates quality?

12. How much <u>less</u> does the other product cost?

$ _____

How long do you plan to keep this product? _____ years

Do you realize that is only a difference of 25 cents per day to have the best!

Can't you afford 25 cents per day to own the finest?

13. _____

_____

_____

14. _____

_____

_____

OBJECTION #28

"Give Me a 10 Percent Discount, and I'll Buy Today."

1. **You know, when I started my business, I decided to always quote my best price first.**

This is the only way I can maintain my integrity.

I FIGURE IT IS BETTER TO APOLOGIZE FOR MY COMMITMENT TO QUALITY ONLY ONCE THAN TO BE FORCED TO APOLOGIZE ABOUT POOR WORKMANSHIP FOREVER.

2. **If you give me an order for 10, I can give you a 10 percent discount.**

If you order only one, you need to pay the same price that all my customers pay.

WOULD YOU LIKE TO ORDER 10?

3. (Prospect's name), **our price is based upon our high-quality materials, superior design, excellent workmanship, and durability.**

That's exactly where your discount will come from.

YOU'LL SAVE MORE THAN 10
PERCENT ON OUR PRODUCT OVER
ITS LIFETIME BECAUSE OF FEWER
REPAIRS, LOWER MAINTENANCE,
AND FEWER HEADACHES.

Can we write your order now?

4. **If there were a less expensive method** of
producing the product you want, we would be
the first to propose it.

We build at the lowest possible cost and
sell at the lowest possible price.

NOW THAT YOU UNDERSTAND
THAT, CAN WE PLACE YOUR ORDER?

5. (Prospect's name), we build our product up to
a certain quality standard—not down to a
price.

We could produce a lower-priced item, but
our experience shows it isn't worth it.

This is a proven design that gives 100
percent satisfaction—not 90 percent.

Now that you understand our commitment to quality, can we place your order?

6. **Do you give a 10 percent discount on everything you sell?**
No?
Well, we don't either.
Why should you expect us to do something you yourself don't do?
What is your real reason for hesitating?

7. **Does Rolls Royce give discounts?**
No.
We are known as the Rolls Royce of this industry, yet we are already available at bargain prices.
What more could you want??
Can we place your order today?

8. **Would you trust a doctor who offered discounts?**

Would you trust a lawyer who had to give discounts to get your business?
NO.

Well, we consider ourselves professionals.

Like other professionals, we charge a fair rate and <u>we don't give discounts.</u>

<u>Instead, we give top quality service.</u>

Isn't that what you really want?

9. WE HAVE NEVER GIVEN DISCOUNTS IN THE PAST.

WE DO NOT GIVE DISCOUNTS NOW.

WE WILL NEVER GIVE DISCOUNTS IN THE FUTURE.

Now that that is settled, can we write up your order?

10. <u>Are you worried that someone else will get a better price than you?</u>

I can guarantee that will not happen!

Since no one will ever get a lower price or a discount, can we take care of the paperwork and write up your order now?

11. **The price you see here already includes a 20 percent discount!**
OUR REGULAR PRICE IS $_____!
So, <u>you have your discount!</u>
Let's take care of the paperwork and get you this machine!

12. I can't feed my kids on discounts! (<u>Humorously.</u>)

13. **Over 5,000 people have bought our product and no one has ever received a discount.**
Why do you think all these people bought from us?
Would you like to learn how they benefited from our product?

14. _____
        _____
        _____

15. _____
        _____
        _____

OBJECTION #29

"You've Got to Do Better Than That."

1. I understand that you want a lower price, and we will be more than happy to lower it to the level you have in mind.

Let's review the options that you'd like to cut from our proposal, so we can meet your needs.

2. **We are building our product up to a quality, not down to a price.**

A lower price would prevent us from staying in business and serving your needs later on.

<u>When you buy from the cheapest companies in this industry, you are buying from companies that might be out of business next year.</u>

Doesn't that concern you?

Shouldn't you really buy from us?

3. Yes, we can do better than that if you agree to give us a larger order.

4. It was my understanding that we were discussing the sale of our product and not the sale of our business. (<u>Humorously.</u>)

5. <u>I appreciate your sense of humor.</u>

    How much better can you get than rock-bottom?

    YOU SEE, OUR POLICY IS TO QUOTE THE BEST PRICE FIRST.

    We have built our reputation on high quality and integrity—it's the best policy.

6. <u>I'd be glad to give you the names of many of our customers so you can find out exactly how much they paid for our product.</u>

    You'll see it's exactly the same as we are asking you to pay.

    We could not develop our reputation without being fair to everyone.

7. I appreciate the opportunity to do a better selling job.

Obviously, you must have a reason for looking exclusively on the dollar side of our proposal.

Let's review the value that you'll be receiving.

8. I've got to do better than that???

What do you mean by <u>better?</u>

9. I have got to do better than that?

Do you want a longer service warranty?

A lower price?

Extended delivery?

Free updates?

Tell me exactly what you want, and I will do everything I can to please you!

10. "I" have got to do better than that?

<u>Can YOU find any other company that can match what I have proposed??</u>

If you find someone else who can do better, bring it to me, and then we will talk.

I THINK I HAVE ALREADY PROPOSED THE BEST DEAL IN THE BUSINESS!

Why not buy today??

11. You can't do better than perfection.

What is left to improve upon??

12. This same deal has pleased over 2,000 of our corporate clients.

Why isn't it good enough for you?

13. _____

_____

_____

14. _____

_____

_____

OBJECTION #30

"I'm Just Shopping Around."

1. That's great.
You've got to start someplace.
How did you hear about us?

2. Welcome to our place.
Perhaps I can save you time finding what you may be looking for.
If there was an ideal solution, how would you describe it?

3. Of course you do. I encourage that.
Let me ask you a question. What other products have you considered that might fit your situation?

4. Great. I am glad you told me that.
What are some of the features that you are looking for in particular?

5. Wonderful. Are you shopping for yourself or for someone special?

6. **You came to the right place.**

We have just about every model in inventory ready for you to look at.

And if you don't see what we have here in the store, we can get it for you in a matter of days.

7. **Thank you for giving us the opportunity to show you our current selection.**

I'd like you to know that we take pride in our quality service.

Are you shopping for yourself or for someone in your family?

8. **That's terrific. Out of curiosity, what made you decide to come to our place?**

9. **We encourage shopping around.** I was wondering what are some of the things that you are looking for?

10. We are happy to have you.

You'll be pleased to know that during a typical week, we have over 200 people visit us to shop around.

If I may ask, when was the last time that you shopped for a _____? (Wait for answer.)

Oh, yes, there have been many changes in that field since then. Can you tell me more about what you expect from a _____.

11. It is not an easy job to shop around in today's market. So many products, so many options.

I can help you take some of the stress out of shopping around.

May I ask you what's most important to you: features, price of, ease of handling?

12. That's a good enough reason for me to help you. I enjoy helping people make shopping easier and more fun.

Let me ask you, what's most important to you at this very moment?

13. **I can help you with that.** (<u>Smile.</u>)

I have a Ph.D. in shopping around. What kind of product would you like to look at first?

14. **It is a great day for shopping. Allow me to join you.**

You probably know that we're having a special sale this week.

Did you read about us in the newspaper?

15. **We are thrilled to have you shop with us.**

Since we have about 1,200 different products and services available, I can help you find what you have in mind.

(<u>Pause.</u>) What do you have in mind?

16. **Great. Have you just started, or have you been looking for some time?**

How long have you been looking? (<u>Wait for answer, then probe for needs.</u>)

17. **Shopping for a _____ can be tiring, isn't it?**

If I can help you get what you need at a great price, would you consider making a decision today?

18. **I understand. Are you shopping for a dream, a goal, or a bargain?** I can help you with the last two!

19. **We can help you get what you want.**

What is most important to you today? A quality product at a great price?

20. **You are welcome to shop here as long as you like.**

I want you to feel at home here.
May I get you some coffee, tea, or a bottle of water?

By the way, my name is (say your name here). What is your name?

Well, I want you to know that I'd be delighted to help you shop.

21. _____

_____

_____

22. _____

_____

_____

© Hisham Bharoocha

About the Author

A dual citizen of both Austria and the United States, Gerhard Gschwandtner is the founder and publisher of *Selling Power,* the leading magazine for sales professionals worldwide, with a circulation of 165,000 subscribers in 67 countries.

He began his career in his native Austria in the sales training and marketing departments of a large construction equipment company. In 1972, he moved to the United States to become the company's North American Sales Training Director, later moving into the position of Marketing Manager.

In 1977, he became an independent sales training consultant, and in 1979 created an audiovisual sales training course called "The Languages of Selling." Marketed to sales managers at Fortune 500 companies, the course taught nonverbal communication in sales together with professional selling skills.

In 1981, Gerhard launched *Personal Selling Power,* a tabloid format newsletter directed to sales managers. Over the years the tabloid grew in subscriptions, size, and frequency. The name changed to *Selling Power,* and in magazine format it became the leader in the professional sales field. Every year *Selling Power* publishes the "Selling Power 500," a listing of the 500 largest sales forces in America. The company publishes books, sales training posters, and audio and video products for the professional sales market.

Gerhard has become America's leading expert on selling and sales management. He conducts webinars for such companies as SAP, and *Selling Power* has recently launched a new conference division that sponsors and conducts by-invitation-only leadership conferences directed toward companies with high sales volume and large sales forces.

For more information on *Selling Power* and its products and services, please visit www.sellingpower.com.

Subscribe to *Selling Power* today and close more sales tomorrow!

GET 10 ISSUES – INCLUDING *THE SALES MANAGER'S SOURCE BOOK.*

In every issue of *Selling Power* magazine you'll find:

■ **A Sales Manager's Training Guide** with a one-hour sales training workshop complete with exercises and step-by-step instructions. Get a new guide in every issue! Created by proven industry experts who get $10,000 or more for a keynote speech or a training session.

■ **Best-practices reports** that show you how to win in today's tough market. Valuable tips and techniques for opening more doors and closing more sales.

■ **How-to stories** that help you speed up your sales cycle with innovative technology solutions, so you'll stay on the leading edge and avoid the "bleeding edge."

■ **Tested motivation ideas** so you and your team can remain focused, stay enthusiastic and prevail in the face of adversity.

NEW! Digital Edition same as print. 100% online.

Plus, you can sign up for five online SellingPower.com newsletters absolutely FREE.

FOR FASTEST SERVICE CALL 800-752-7355
TO SUBSCRIBE ONLINE GO TO WWW.SELLINGPOWER.COM

30 Great Strategies for Sales Success ... Fix the Slumping Rep ...

Selling Power
SOLUTIONS FOR SALES MANAGEMENT

Danica Patrick
Racing Ahead

LANCE
Inside the Mind of a Winner

Selling Power®

I want a one-year subscription to *Selling Power* magazine.

☐ **YES!** Send me one year of the print edition for only $27
☐ **YES!** Sign me up for one year of the digital edition for only $19
☐ **YES!** Sign me up for one year of both for only $33

Please note: Subscriptions begin upon receipt of payment. For priority service include check or credit card information. Canadian and overseas subscriptions, please visit www.sellingpower.com for rates.

Name: _____ Title: _____

Company: _____

Address: _____

City: _____ State: _____ Zip: _____ Phone: _____

☐ Check enclosed   Charge my ☐ Visa ☐ MC ☐ AMEX ☐ Discover

Card number: _____ Exp.: _____

Name on card: _____ Signature: _____

For fastest service call 800-752-7355 • To subscribe online go to www.sellingpower.com